The DNA of Internet Marketing

Keeping You Ahead of the Internet Marketing Game

Lehman Hailey

AuthorHouse™
1663 Liberty Drive
Bloomington, IN 47403
www.authorhouse.com
Phone: 1-800-839-8640

Requests for permissions to use portions of this book should be emailed to:
support@lehmanhailey.com

© 2009 Lehman Hailey. All rights reserved.

No part of this book may be reproduced, stored in a retrieval system, or transmitted by any means without the written permission of the author.

First published by AuthorHouse 7/28/2009

ISBN: 978-1-4490-0190-2 (sc)

Printed in the United States of America
Bloomington, Indiana

This book is printed on acid-free paper.

Disclaimer:
The contents of this book are intended as tips and tools for internet marketers and entrepreneurs, based on experience working in the industry, research, and interviews with gurus in the field. The information contained herein is not guaranteed to work for your business. The author and experts quoted in this book offer their advice as suggestions. They cannot be held liable if your situation cannot be resolved through the tips and tools provided. Each internet business is unique and individual. While this book offers excellent ideas to try, you are highly encouraged to seek out multiple sources and references when building your business. The purchaser or reader of this book assumes responsibility for the use of these materials and information. There are no guarantees of any income and the author reserves the right to make changes in the book with no liability whatsoever to the purchasers or readers of this material.

This book is dedicated to my incredible wife Kathleen and my two amazing sons Matthew and Nicholas. I could not ask for a better family!

Special thanks to:

Matt Bacak - http://www.promotingtips.com (Forward)
Russell Brunson - http://www.DotComSecrets.com (Bonus Chapter)
Howie Schwartz - http://www.howiesapprentice.com (Bonus Chapter)
Mike Dillard - http://www.MagneticSponsoring.com (Bonus Chapter)

I want to thank each one of you for everything you do for this industry as well as taking the time out of your very busy schedule to contribute to this book.

Table of Contents

INTRODUCTION ix

FOREWORD xiii

CHAPTER ONE 1
    Establishing Your Target Market

CHAPTER TWO 11
    Squeeze Pages and Branding Sites

CHAPTER THREE 21
    PPC Google – Yahoo – MSN

CHAPTER FOUR 31
    Article Marketing

CHAPTER FIVE 37
    Video Marketing and Podcasting

CHAPTER SIX 43
    Press Releases

CHAPTER SEVEN 49
    Web 2.0 and Social Marking Sites

CHAPTER EIGHT 57
    Outsourcing

CHAPTER NINE 63
    Marketing Resources

BONUS CHAPTER 73

RUSSELL BRUNSON: FIRE FIRST, AIM LATER

BONUS CHAPTER – HOW TO GET $50,000/MO IN ONLINE ADVERTISING FOR FREE… 81

BY MIKE DILLARD

BONUS CHAPTER 87

HOWIE SCHWARTZ

CONCLUSION 93

TAKE ACTION!

Introduction

Hi, I'm Lehman Hailey. For many years, I owned a successful mortgage company. I had offices in two states and 40 loan officers working for me. I was making a lot of money and my business was very successful, but I was also chained to my work. I didn't have time to travel and enjoy my life, and I didn't have free time to spend with my wife and children. The way it turned out, my business owned me every bit as much as I owned the business.

I knew I needed a change – that I needed to shift my entrepreneurial spirit in another direction. In 2004, I decided to focus on building a home business. My goals were fairly simple: I wanted to make more money than I was making in the mortgage industry, and I wanted to do it with time left over each day to spend with my family. Within six months, I was able to close my mortgage company, had more than replaced my income, and had more free time than I knew what to do with. In fact, in one single month I made more than $75,000 – more than most people make in a year!

I've spent the last four years turning my home business into a thriving internet venture. Along the way, I've learned nearly everything there is to know about internet marketing and how to use the internet as a tool to build not just wealth but freedom. I spend most of my time talking to other internet marketers, doing research, and staying as up-to-date as possible on the newest tools and resources in internet marketing and then share what I learn with my partners and customers.

I want everyone to find the kind of success and happiness I've found, and that's why I've written this book, exposing internet marketing secrets that can help you build and grow your business quickly. I know from experience that internet marketing is a powerful tool, but that you can spend a lot of time and money trying to figure out how to make it work for you.

Just like any tool, internet marketing is a tool that needs to come with a set of step-by-step instructions. My book can help you whether you are a brand new entrepreneur or an experienced internet guru. Inside this book, you will find tips and tools to help you unlock the secrets of successful internet marketing. This isn't just some vague set of instructions, either; it's a detailed instruction manual designed to help you be the most successful YOU that you can possibly be.

I am humbled by the fact that people consider me an expert in internet marketing and direct sales. I learned the hard way and made a lot of mistakes along the way – but I also met some amazing people, like Matt Bacak, whose energy and positivity helped me believe in the possibilities, and like Russell Brunson and Mike Dillard, whose stories you'll read about later in the book.

Being able to leave a business – a business that tied me down and forced me to spend more time slaving away than I ever wanted to spend – was the best day of my life. I'm sharing my success secrets with you because I want you to be able to experience that moment, to take control of your own destiny.

Foreword

There is only one way to stay in business in this new, economically restructured climate. It's simple, really: you have to be online to survive. More than that, you have to know how to use the Internet as a tool to drive targeted customers to your website and know how to provide perceived value in order to get those customers to stay.

It's not about being the oldest business in town anymore – we've seen plenty of those fail; businesses most consumers thought would be capable of surviving anything. No, what you have to be to survive in this century is flexible, nimble, quick on your feet. You need to be able to read the metrics on your website and instantly respond to the direction your customers need you to go in.

It's no longer the fast-food way of doing business, offering the same cheeseburger to every customer regardless of which drive-thru they are in; it's about establishing yourself as a credible presence, developing a customer base who believes in what you are delivering and always hungry for what you are offering.

When you recognize the power of the internet and learn how to use it properly, you will: expand your reach further and explode your business quickly.

We have come to a time where you won't have success in this century if you don't understand internet marketing…and you can't understand internet marketing if you don't read the powerful information inside Lehman Hailey's book.

What I admire most about Lehman is that he has been out there in the trenches using internet marketing and making it work for him. Instead of selling you a line of bull or trying to steer you in the wrong direction, he's sharing secrets he's learned doing it day in and day out. If you really want to know what it takes to be a part of this groundbreaking shift in business building, Lehman is THE INTERNET MARKETING EXPERT. He's been out there doing this stuff, using the same stuff he's telling you to use in this book.

Lehman is sharing his own amazing success with his readers, knowing that they are just as capable – with the right tools and information – of building a successful, moneymaking internet business. He lets you inside his head; he shares the secrets of the industry. It's almost shocking how he lays open internet marketing and dissects it.

The DNA of Internet Marketing can turn an internet newbie into a self-sufficient, web entrepreneur with a future that no longer depends on a corporate structure or the approval of a board of directors; this book can turn internet marketing pros into internet sensations well on their way to earning their first billion.

I know what I'm talking about, because I've known Lehman Hailey for over five years. I've watched him grow not one but two businesses into amazing successes, earning more in one month than most people earn in a year, using the same secrets he is sharing with you in this amazing book.

The information you will find inside this book will astonish you. Not only is it a simple-to-use, step by step BIBLE for building a business on the internet, but the strategies Lehman shares with you are PROVEN to help you find success.

READING THIS BOOK CAN MEAN THE DIFFERENCE BETWEEN A MEDIOCRE EXISTENCE AND EXTRAVAGENT LIVING. This book will give you the tools to launch your internet business quickly, cost-effectively, and with more success than you thought possible.

It is an authentic, realistic guide to success. The information in this book reveal secrets that I'm not sure other internet marketers are going to appreciate having revealed…Lehman truly bares all and strips away any of the secrecy surrounding true internet marketing success and gives you every tool you need to be making money RIGHT NOW.

Lehman Hailey

Do yourself a favor. Stop what you are doing. Read this book cover to cover. Take notes. Follow the steps Lehman gives you. I am confident you can launch a new business or improve an existing business and BUILD WEALTH using the internet marketing secrets inside this book.

Matt Bacak

Chapter One

Establishing Your Target Market

One of the most common questions that I have gotten over the past several years is "How do you successfully marketing your business online?" Establishing you target market is probably the most important thing you can do when getting your business started. The reason you want to establish your target market is to zero in on who your customers really are. If you do not know the make up of your customers, then you will be throwing money out the window when it comes to ANY type of marketing.

Let me give you an example. A few years ago, I had a client/business partner ask me about a few ways to marketing on the internet. After showing them exactly what to do and how to get their ads out there for their market to see they decided to take the easy road… or so it seemed. Instead of going out and doing their research and doing the due diligence on who their target was, they decided to cast a net over the whole ocean and see what they caught.

First of all, let me tell you that working any business like this will put you out of business very fast. Yes, you will get some prospects/leads that will come through your marketing efforts, and they might even be good prospects/leads. The problem is that you threw your marketing out for everyone to see. If you are doing any paid type of marketing you won't be do it for long.

Marketing to the wrong set of keywords will KILL your business, produce a substandard leads, and will suck you bank account dry. You just don't throw everything against the wall and see what sticks. On the other hand, marketing to the right set of keywords or the right target market will EXPLODE your business. Believe it or not, there really is a systematic approach to marketing a business online. So you might be to the point now where you are saying to yourself, "How do I establish my target market and how do I find the right keywords or key phrases in order to zero in on my potential customers?"

Well, the first thing that I do is get out a pen and paper and start to write down the top 10 words that relate to what my business, product, or service is all about. Remember that while you are thinking about words that relate to what you are marketing you should also be thinking about phrases. Here is an example of what I am talking about. Let's say that you are marketing left-handed golf clubs. Your focus should not only be on keywords like golf clubs but the whole phrase "Left Handed Golf Clubs." By having phrases that match exactly what you are offering will drastically increase the quality of your prospects/leads.

Establishing your target market is huge. Understanding your target market is the first step in internet marketing. Using google is one of the easiest ways to find out who your target will be for your online business. There are some questions that you will need to ask yourself when researching your target market. You need to be able to answer the following questions:

- Who is your customer
- What do they do
- What is their age group
- Where do they live
- Where do they hang out

Think of as many of these types of questions as possible and answer them about your customers. This will help you establish the target market that you're looking for. Think of as many questions as you can about your target market and write them down. The more you can know about your target market, the better you will be able to personalize your marketing to reach the segment of the population most likely to want your products and services.

Keywords and Their Impact on Target Marketing

Part of developing your target market is by understanding keywords and how they work for you. Keywords are the words search engines pick up from your web site that make it show up in internet searches on various search engines. When you are doing pay-per-click or targeted marketing, you're going to have to have certain keywords that are targeted to the type of people that you're looking for.

If you're marketing on Yahoo, Google, MSN, etc., you need keywords to market to. Let's say you're in a home business, direct sales oriented, and you're looking for people to market to, people who want to work from home. You need the right keywords, and the more of those keywords you have, the more of those people you will attract. Words like internet business, online business, home based business, home business, business opportunity. The more popular the keyword or keyword phrase, the more competitive it is going to be.

Keyword Tools

So as you establish your target market, try to get into some areas that might not be as highly competitive – a niche – and corner that market. Now you're going to need a tool to mine these keywords, to find the keywords and keyword phrases you need, to put into your campaign that you're going to be marketing to, you're going to need a tool. This is your keyword research for target marketing. One of the tools that I go to first when I am looking into a niche market is a tool called **Spyfu.com**. Spyfu is a great tool to use when looking into the keywords and key phrases your competition is targeting. Not only can you research keywords and key phrases, you can type in a web address (maybe a competitors site) and research the exact keywords and phrases that they are marketing on. This tool is great research and will shorten your learning curve when working on finding your target market.

The DNA of Internet Marketing

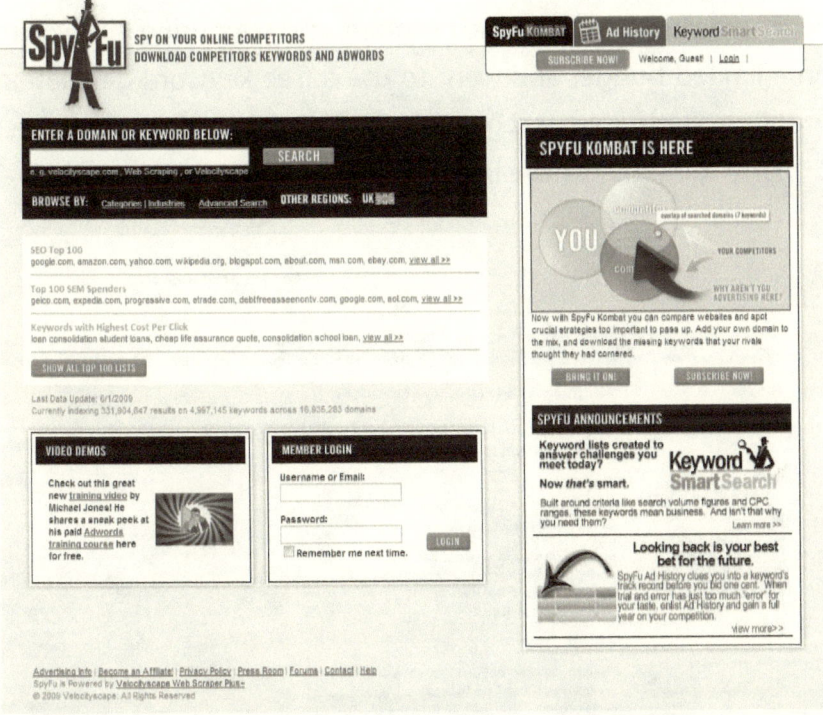

Another free keyword tool – probably one of the best free ones, because you can generate misspelled keywords – is **goodkeywords.com**. Let me explain what I mean about misspelled keywords. A lot of times, when people go to do a search on the internet, they are typing so fast that they type the search term in wrong. They misspell them. This site will help you come up with the most common misspellings of the keywords and search terms you want to use.

For example, with the word home business, one of the most common misspellings is o-m-e business. They are typing so fast that the "h" doesn't work. Ome business becomes a legitimate keyword, one you can bid on. It's very cheap and it's a good way to get leads. If you want to use this keyword tool, you'll need to download it to your hard drive, open up the program, and start using it. If you're on a limited budget and want to use a free keyword generating program, Spyfu.com and goodkeywords.com are two of the best 3rd party tools that I have used.

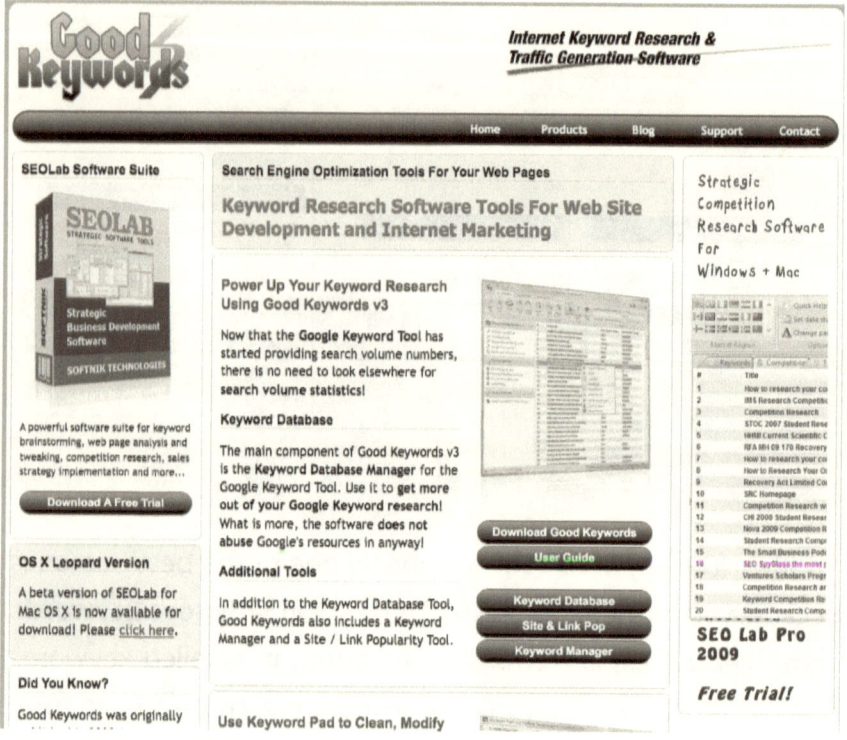

If you want to use paid programs, adwordsaccelerator.com is about $37 a month. It's a good program, the one I choose to use. It lays everything out for you. You can go to the website and watch a demo of their services.

The DNA of Internet Marketing

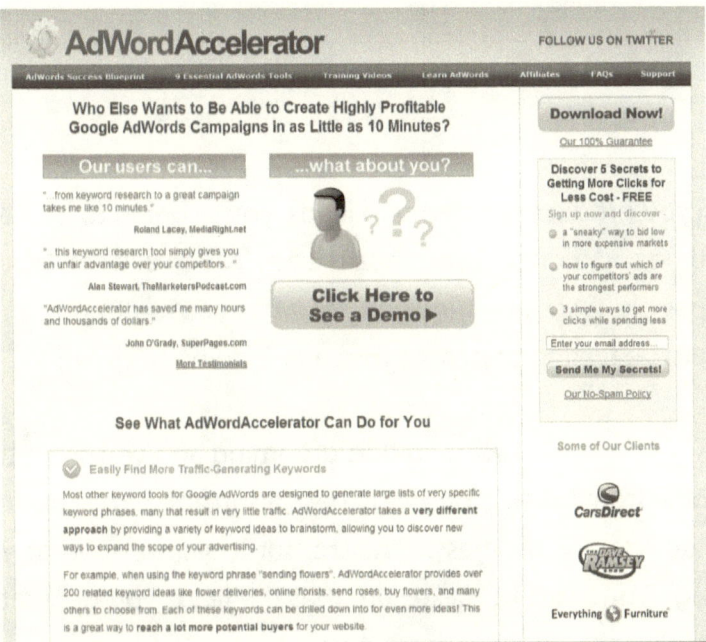

Keywords, then, are the foundation of your business.

<u>**Marketing to the wrong set of keywords will suck your bank account dry!**</u>

I've seen people conduct internet marketing campaigns on Google and spend $1500 in about an hour and a half or two hours. They get discouraged and don't want to do it anymore and they quit, because they can't afford it. I've seen people have their bank accounts sucked dry from marketing the wrong way on the internet, so you don't want to market to the wrong keywords.

Keywords are the foundation of your business. You have to make sure you're marketing to highly targeted keywords and that you know exactly what you're doing and how to manage your internet marketing.

Marketing to the wrong set of keywords will produce substandard leads!

When you produce substandard leads, you're going to be wasting both time and money. Substandard leads lead to bad conversations with people who aren't looking for what you're offering. You're going to be talking to people who aren't going to convert.

Let's say you're marketing to dog grooming and you get a bunch of people from horse grooming, that's a substandard lead. It's not targeted to your business. They're not looking for what you're offering. You want to make sure that the leads you generate are ones really looking for your product.

If you're in the sports industry and you sell sports-related equipment, you want to make sure that everyone who is coming to your site, everyone who is clicking on your ads pertains to sports industry and sports equipment.

Marketing to the wrong set of keywords will kill your business!

Over the last several years, I've seen this happen a number of times. People fall off because they do not know how to market and they market to the wrong target market. Learn to market to the correct target market. Find out what your market is and market to that target only. Don't scatter your marketing efforts to all these different areas on the internet and expect to get good, quality leads. You need to have quality, targeted leads.

Another free tool that you should be using is Google's keyword generator, at https://adwords.google.com/select/KeywordToolExternal?defaultView=2. This is Google's keyword tool. It's free and it is the one that I use most of the time. It won't do misspellings, but if you're marketing on Google, this is a great one to use, because it gives you a really great breakdown of the keyword searches.

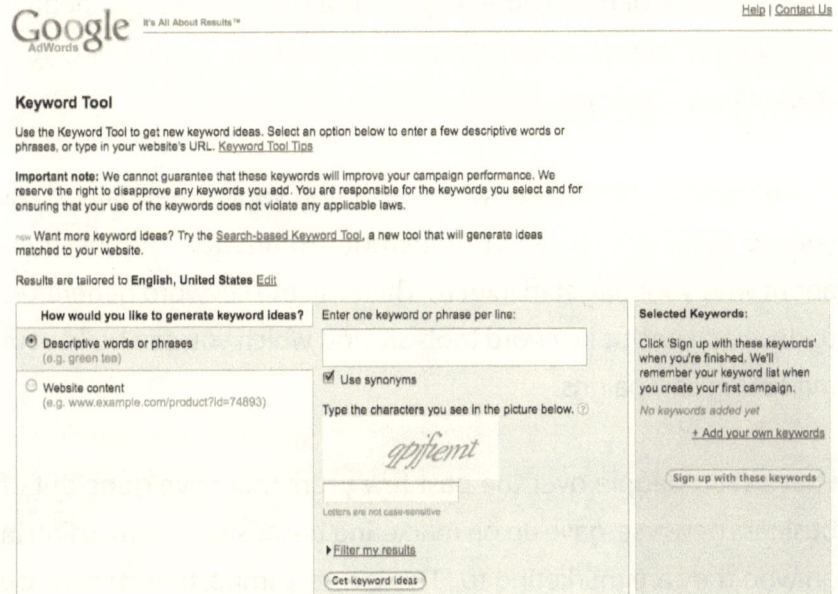

The way this tool works is that you can enter a specific keyword phrase, like internet marketing. Enter the security code and then click "get more keywords." Google generates a list of related keywords, the search volume, and the level of competition you will have with each keyword. Google's keywords can help you find keywords you can use both with marketing on Google as well as marketing with other sites and search engines.

This is a great tool for mining for keywords that people click on. You can build campaigns around these keywords. You can copy and paste the list of words into a text or .csv file or paste it into a spreadsheet and then use the words in your marketing efforts.

You can use Google's keyword tool to generate ideas for keywords. Try searching for other words related to internet marketing, like promoting, or marketing tips, or promoting your business. You'll see that some of these other keywords are a little less competitive and can provide you with different alternatives for building your marketing campaigns.

Using these keywords is how you establish your target market. As you do this, make sure you remember to answer the questions about who your target market is. Then use the keyword generators to develop specific keyword tools around which you can build your marketing campaigns.

I have seen people over the past few years that have gone out of business or worse, gave up on marketing because of not focusing in on who they are marketing to. This is a very important step in you journey to becoming a great internet marketer. The people that set themselves up the right way in the beginning are the ones that end up being ultra successful and it all starts with knowing how to establish your target market.

Chapter Two

Squeeze Pages and Branding Sites

Now that we have established our target market and know who it is that we are wanting to attract to our site we now need to make a decision on the type of site that we are wanting to use. Squeeze pages and branding sites are different, but both are necessary tools for the internet marketer. As with any other topic, you will get different opinions when it comes to Squeeze Pages or Branding sites. Personally, I would do both.

There are marketing techniques that I use only my squeeze page on and others where I only use my branding site. The squeeze page is the most important page you are going to create. It is the first page you should create in your marketing campaign and the fastest way to collect business partners and leads. A squeeze page is a mini sales page. Squeeze pages are also called opt in pages, splash pages, and flycatcher pages.

Squeeze pages are short, to the point, and designed to get the customer to give you their contact information. The information on your squeeze page should grab the person's attention and get them to give you at least a first name and an email address. A basic squeeze page outline has an eye-grabbing headline, four to six bulleted points, an obvious opt-in, and a tempting giveaway. Squeeze pages are named for their goal of squeezing information out of the person. The goal of the squeeze page is to get your customer's interest piqued so high that they have to find out what else you have to say.

This is why the squeeze page is the most important page that you will be creating in your marketing campaign. It's the best way to get a lot of leads coming through the door.

Designing Your Squeeze Page

The headline at the top should be red or maroon and should create interest. The bullets should be nice and bright. They are enticing. They are meant to pique the reader's interest, not give them the full information. They should tease them and get them to the next page. They should hint at what they will find out *after* they opt in.

The call to action is exactly what it says. It calls your customer to take action. It gets them to fill in the form and opt in. It says, "Do this to get this." What are they going to get by filling in their name and email address? "Fill in your name and primary email address to get this free newsletter…free video…free audio." There should be something you give away that is a call to action to get them to go further on.

A squeeze page cuts through all the junk that is ongoing in your customer's life and gets their attention. You are a problem solver with your squeeze page. Your squeeze page is wrapped around your product or service. You have to know your customers wants needs and desires before creating your squeeze page. There are no short cuts for this.

When a squeeze page is put together the right way, it can attract an enormous amount of leads. The best squeeze pages:

- Invoke curiosity. They have an intriguing story that compels people to opt in. They capture the lead. Building your list is one of the most important things you can do with your squeeze page, because your list is a group you can always market to.
- Have a hook. They contain a promise to insider information or secrets that have never been revealed before. They offer something you can hook your customer with to get them to sign up.
- Have a motivating call to action. They offer something of value in exchange for the contact information you request. A good squeeze page will make your customers feel like they are missing something if they don't sign up.

Example Squeeze Page

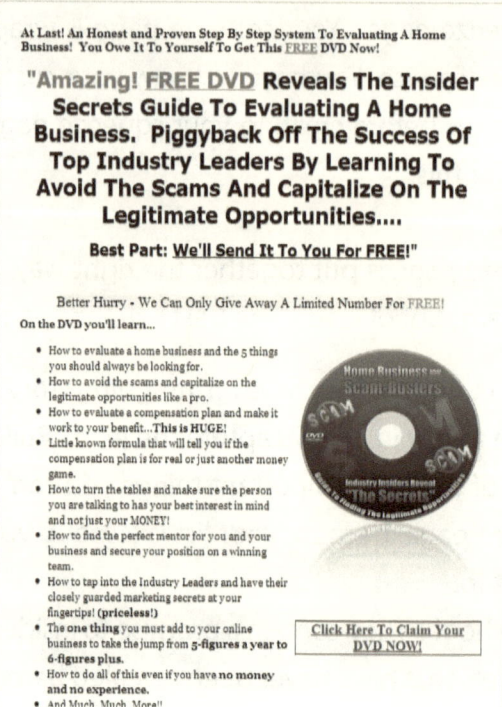

The headline should invoke curiosity:

"AMAZING FREE DVD REVEALS THE INSIDER SECRETS GUIDE TO EVALUATING HOME BUSINESS. Piggy back off the success of top industry leaders by learning to avoid the scams and capitalize on the legitimate opportunities..."

The bullet points should pique curiosity without giving away too much information:

- 10 Ways to Discover a Scam
- How to Make the Most of Your Investment

The DNA of Internet Marketing

The call to action tells the customer what they must do NOW:

You better hurry – we can only give away a limited number of DVDs for free!

The opt-in prompts them for a name, primary email address, and sometimes a phone number.

At the bottom, there might even be a better hook, like a free 30-minute coaching call if they act now.

Creating Your Squeeze Page Headline

A great way to really get out there and learn how to create your own headline for your squeeze page is to start with typing in keywords for your industry. Go to your competitors' pages. Find headlines that fit your market. Take them, copy them, then reword them to fit your business. I don't mean steal someone else's headline. I mean analyze the headlines, read what other people are doing, and implement some of the trigger words that they are using.

You will have to test multiple headlines. If you're not getting the results you want, test another headline. You will find that you will need to test over and over. Some headlines you think will work won't; some that you wouldn't think would will. Your headlines should be in quotes. Some proven headline templates include:

- "Who else wants to …"
- "You're about to learn the secrets that most …"
- "Do you make these … mistakes?"

Bullet Points

Bullets allow your potential customer to skim through what you're offering. They're a way for you to entice the customer to opt in by teasing them with enough information to make them want more.

You can swipe bullets, too, just like you do headlines. Use the trigger words that you see having success, and rewrite them to suit your industry and your product. Numbered bullets, secret bullets, how to bullets…all of these grab the reader and pique their curiosity. Successful templates for bullet points include:

- Number Bullets
- Huge Benefit Bullets
- Secret Bullets
- Exclusive Bullets
- How To Bullets

Fill in the blank with your product or service. Remember, you should have four to six bullet points on your squeeze page. They should be highlights of what they are going to get if they opt in. They should invoke curiosity.

Call to Action

The call to action is down at the bottom, close to where your customer will fill in their information. The call to action is very important. It tells your customers exactly what they need to do.

A good call to action should say, "Enter your name and primary email address to…

- receive your free gift
- get your free dvd
- get a free 30-minute coaching call
- get your free report on…

Giving away something will increase your opt ins dramatically. You can't just give away anything; it has to be something of value if you want them to become a buying customer. You can even tell your customers how much the free item is worth (for example, a 30-minute coaching call might be worth $200). Always include a message at the bottom of your squeeze page that you will not sell or rent their information to anyone else.

Branding Sites

Branding sites are designed to brand YOU. For branding sites, I use WordPress sites. Google likes WordPress. I recommend outsourcing the development and writing of your WordPress site, since your time can be better spent developing your products and services.

WordPress sites are great for branding. WordPress sites have a home page. The home page allows you to provide more information and detail than a squeeze page. The branding site is meant to give people information – lots of information about you, your product, and your services.

Lay out your branding site with a home page about your product and service. The "about me" tab should be all about you…your story, your history, your information. It gives your customers a connection to you before you even call or email them.

You can also add more tabs, including a blog. A blog is a great way to add content to your website. As you add content, Google comes and crawls your site and sees the new information on your branding site. That's why Google likes these WordPress sites so much – because the content can change all the time.

Example Branding Site:

On your branding site, the minimum information you will have is a home page, an about me page, and a blog. You should blog three or four times a week about the subject, service or product (the blogging can also be outsourced, particularly if you're not a good writer). You can add additional tabs as well. For example, if your site is a golf product, you can expand your tabs and have golf tips, golf coaching, a section on putting and a section on driving. As you can see, your branding site can really expand on what and who you are.

From your branding site, you can have links to your social networking sites. You will also have on your branding site an opt-in form with the same free giveaway from your squeeze page. Your ultimate goal, even with the branding site, is still to generate leads. Give your site visitors something of value to get their contact information.

Driving Traffic to Your Sites

There are multiple ways to drive traffic to your squeeze page and your branding site. While most traffic driving tools are appropriate for both, pay-per-click ad campaigns should only be used to drive traffic to your squeeze page. They are expensive to use, so don't waste time with anything less than the best leads.

In addition to pay per click, you can drive traffic to your sites by:

- Natural ranking. The more information you have on your website and the more you blog and write articles on your site, the more your natural rank will increase.
- SEO. Search-engine optimized writing can drive traffic to both your squeeze page and your branding site. While it is easier to drive traffic to your branding site with SEO, you can rank a squeeze page by using well-placed keywords and content.
- Banner and texts ads. You can drive traffic from banner and text ads to either your squeeze page or your branding site.
- Offline marketing. Again, you can drive traffic to either site.

- Email marketing. While you can drive email traffic to either site, you will probably generate more leads if you drive the traffic to your squeeze page.
- Traffic exchange also works for either, but I don't do a lot of traffic exchange.
- Co-registration. I also do not use co-registration, but if I do, I send them to my squeeze page.
- Web 2.0 (Facebook, MySpace, Twitter, etc). I link to both my branding site and my squeeze page.
- Article marking. I do drive some to my squeeze page, but I primarily send them to my branding site.
- Blogging. I drive traffic to both my branding site and my squeeze page with my blog.
- Press releases. Especially paid press releases submitted through PR Web I use to drive traffic to both sites.

***

Squeeze pages and branding sites both have their purpose, but if you're just launching, the squeeze page should be the priority. Squeeze pages are short, to the point, and meant to grab leads. Put your squeeze page to work for you NOW. While you're driving traffic to the squeeze page, you can start building your branding site and blogging to generate more traffic. A branding site is meant to brand you as a leader in your industry. You can combine the two by having a call to action and offering your free giveaway on your branding site.

Chapter Three

PPC Google – Yahoo – MSN

Pay Per Click Marketing is the fastest way to drive traffic to your web site, period. The three big pay per click sites that we recommend are as follows and they are in this order for a reason with Google being at the top.

Google Adwords - adwords.google.com
Yahoo Search - searchmarketing.yahoo.com
MSN Ad center - adcenter.microsoft.com

Google is the main pay per click marketing search engine. There are other places that you can market on pay per click. The three major search engines are Google, Yahoo, and MSN, but Google controls most of the market.

How Does Pay Per Click Work?

Pay Per Click works by you selecting keywords that are related to your business, product, or service.

1. You choose keywords or key phrases
2. You bid on those keywords or key phrases to get them seen
3. Google determines which ads to show

So how do you get your ads seen?

1. Write a great ad (great copywriting is a key factor in all marketing)
2. Bid the right amount
3. Make your ad relevant to your keywords as well as your website

I do not want to make it sound to easy but it's really is not that difficult to get your ads seen when you know what you are doing. To many people rush to get their ads out on Google and do not do the proper research, or work with experienced marketers and coaches.

You can apply the strategies you use for Google to Yahoo and MSN. Google's pay per click program is called Ad Words. There is a difference between "natural" searches – the search results that appear on the left-hand side of the search page and the "paid" search results that appear on the top and right-hand side.

Where The Results Are Found

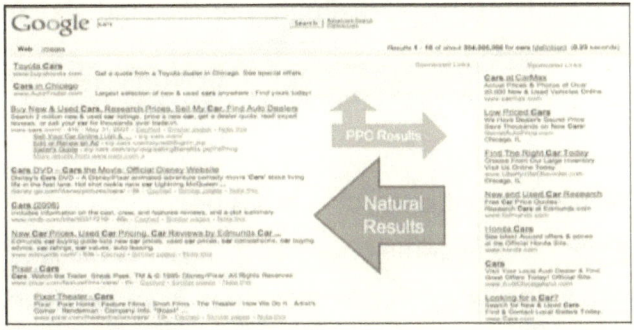

How Search Engines Work

When someone types in a search term, it goes to the Google web server. Google processes the search through both the Search Index servers (natural) and the Ad Word (pay per click) servers as well as the Google web document server before displaying the results, which appear as in the image above.

A Google AdWord can be likened to a three-line classified ad that appears in a newspaper – except that instead of reaching a small audience of classified ad readers, you have the opportunity to reach millions of people by marketing this way on the internet. You get charged every time someone clicks each time someone clicks on your pay per click advertising.

When you are writing these ads, you have a limited number of words and characters. That's why it's so important that you know who your target market is and what keywords you should be using to attract them, so that you get the most out of your three lines on the right-hand side and generate real leads. The ads should be attractive to your target market.

Pay Per Click Definitions

<u>Maximum Cost Per Click</u> – Maximum per click bid you are willing to pay

<u>Impressions</u> – The number of times your pay per click ad has been viewed

<u>Click</u> – The number of times your ad has been clicked

<u>Cost per Click</u> – The average price per click you actually paid

<u>CTR (Click-Through Rate)</u> – Amount of times an ad has been viewed/ Amount of times an ad has been clicked

<u>Creative</u> – Advertisement being distributed

Why Google?

The reason your focus should be on Google versus other search engines is that the majority of people use Google for their searches. Google holds nearly 70% of the market share; if you're not advertising on Google, you might as well not bother advertising. Google is where you want to start.

Google also has the most searches, but they also have the most tutorials to help you use their AdWords tools successfully. Google is flexible, offers the fastest service for campaign and editorial review, and the most features and parameters for ad distribution. You can get your ad up and running very fast. Some of the others, like Yahoo and MSN, have a longer, more drawn out process for getting your ad approved.

How Pay Per Click Works

Pay per click is a keyword bidding system. You're going to establish your target market and what your target market it. Then you will generate keywords or key phrases that pertain to your target market. When you put those keywords and key phrases into Google AdWords, you'll be able to bid on those keywords and key phrases. Depending on your bid and the relevance of your website and the popularity of your ad, your ad will appear further up in the rankings on the pay per click ads and determine your position.

You'll be able to analyze the performance of your Pay Per Click ads by looking at the metrics on your Google account. It will show you your keywords and keyword phrases, your bids, your impressions, your clicks, your CTRs, and your average cost per click. You can run more than one ad at the same time marketing the same keywords to test which one works better and earns a better click-through ratio. If you're testing two ads, give them at least a week. Make sure there's a decent volume running through them. By testing ads this way, you come up with very effective ads. Once you develop an ad that works, throw away the non-performing ad and then develop another one to test against the winning ad. You might be surprised – some ads that you think are home-run winners might not work at all, and ones you don't think will do well do great. Use the Google tutorials, too. They can really help.

Creating Your Ad

Your ad needs to grab your target market. You have very few words and characters to get their attention. Use your keywords in your headline. For example, if you are marketing sports equipment, and your keyword is sports equipment, use the phrase sports equipment in the top line. Talk about the benefits of your product or service in the second line and put a call to action in the third line.

The first line has to be able to draw your target's attention and contain words you know they are looking for. The second line has to make them believe that clicking on the link will benefit them. The third line should clinch the deal, so to speak, and tell them to come visit your site or squeeze page. You really want to get the person to click on your ad and come to your site.

Top Business Opportunity
Top Business Opportunity Exposed
Learn the Secrets of the Wealthy
www.xxxx.com

When you are designing your ad, remember you are trying to target your specific market, the people who are looking for you and what you have to offer. You don't want to waste money by bringing people to your site who have no interest in what you provide; you have to take the time to understand your target market and develop appropriate keywords before designing your ad.

Once you have created your ad, you need to set the parameters of the ad and where you want it to run. Google allows you to distribute your ad locally, nationally, or internationally. You can choose what languages the ad runs in, what days the ad runs. You can set a budget for the ad and even choose what networks your ad is shown on.

As you set up your Google pay per click (PPC) account, the parameters you set will help you drive in more highly targeted traffic, give you more control over your budget, more control over your money – your money is being better spent. It saves you money to do this.

Targeting by country – I do this; you can select which countries you want to market to, and even what cities and regions.

This is a huge tool. Let's say you are a mortgage broker or real estate agent; you can target your ads only to the areas in which you work. All of your leads will be coming from those areas. You can actually put in a latitude and longitude and get very specific about who you target.

Why Should I Use Pay Per Click?

- You are in control of how much traffic you get and how much you pay for it
- You can get targeted traffic to your site quickly
- No long-term commitment – you can start and stop anytime with a click of a button
- You only pay when someone clicks your ad and comes to your site
- Ability to get your site exposure at the expense of others
- You can compete with bigger companies
- You can be better at PPC than bigger companies – the playing field is level
- By gaining traffic through your PPC, you can get a better idea of which keywords you should optimize (SEO)

How to Set Up Your Google AdWords Account

1. Go to Google.com and click on advertising programs
2. Click on Google AdWords
3. Click start now
4. Choose the standard edition and click continue

5. Choose the language you want your ad to come in, and
6. Choose where you want to advertise: countries and territories, regions and cities, or custom; click continue
7. Choose which specific areas you want to add to your locations, then continue
8. Create your ad. Take your time.
    a. Note that the maximum number of characters (that is letters and spaces together) in your headline cannot exceed 25 and the two description lines can only have 35 characters.
    b. Use Google's keyword tool to determine keywords to use in your headline.
    c. Your keyword should be in your headline and in one of the description lines.
    d. The display URL is the link that will be displayed. It doesn't have to be the actual URL with the www.
    e. Your destination URL, however, has to have the www.
    f. Before clicking continue, click on the link to make sure it works properly.
9. Choose your keywords. If it's your first campaign, use just a few keywords to start out with. These keywords should pertain to your business and be highly specific to your target market. Click continue.
10. Choose your budget. You can set a limit and once that limit has been reached, your ad will stop running. Also set the CPC limit – the amount you are willing to pay for someone to click your ad. Try different methods – paying more for CPC may move you up the ranking faster. Choose whatever budget makes you feel comfortable. Your bid for CPCs will

have to be higher if it's a more competitive market, like home business, and will be less expensive if your market is something like basket weaving. Click continue.
11. Review your pay per click order. Make sure your link works. Make any changes you want to make, answer the questions, then click "continue to sign up."
12. If you already have a gmail account or use other Google services, you can use the same username and password for your PPC account. If you do not already use other Google services, it will help you set up a username and password.

Once you've set up your account, you can develop more than one ad to test. You can review the results in the Google summary (choose the "summary" tab). In the summary, you will find detailed information about the number of clicks, impressions, the CTR, the average cost per click, and other pulse-taking details about the account. You can click on the keyword tab to determine which keywords are working well for you.

TIP: Think about what your market is going to see when they run a search. Let's say they are searching for home business. Everywhere the words "home business" appear, they'll be bolded. So, the more often the search term appears in your ad, the more bold words will attract them. A little trick we use is to make sure our "display" URL has the keywords in it, even if the destination URL is something else. For example, if my keyword is home business, even if my destination URL is actually www.lehmanhailey.com, in the display URL, I can add the keyword: lehmanhailey.com/homebusiness. Now be careful when using this technique as google has actually cracked down on this so you ad might not get approved. I know plenty of people that are still using this technique today and I actually use it on a daily basis.

I urge you to watch the Google tutorial videos and use the tools they offer. You can run reports on nearly anything you can imagine.

Conversion Tracking

Under the campaign management tab in your Google PPC account, you need to set up conversion tracking. In order to track conversions, you need to add code to your thank you page. You may need your web designer to help you with this if you don't understand HTML. You want the tracking code put into the thank you page, and Google has a PDF set up guide that you can use or send to your programmer so that they can do it.

To get your conversion page code, go to the campaign management tab, find the AdWord tracking box, and click "get conversion page code." This will take you to a page where you have more choices in determining what your conversion report tells you; you want to choose the box that says "lead." Click continue. It will take you to a page where you can customize, but I typically just leave the standard settings and click continue. On the bottom of the page you will find the HTML code that you need to add to your thank you page. Click inside the box and it will select all of the text. Right-click your mouse and choose copy. Paste that into an email message to your programmer or add it to your thank you page.

Chapter Four

Article Marketing

Article marketing is probably one of our favorite and most effective ways to market. This is not a marketing method that is going to get you traffic tonight. This is something that builds; it takes time, but it is viral. What happens when you do article marketing is that people pick up your articles for content on their sites, for content. It's huge. Your content is spread around virally.

The way this works is you write an article, something of value. Be sure you check out our chapter on outsourcing, because article writing is something you shouldn't waste a lot of time on yourself if you don't like to write, aren't good at writing, you can find someone else to do it for you. But you get these articles written and submitted, and what you are doing is putting in your links on these articles, the articles that you produce. These are one-way links to your site, so when people pick up your articles for content, the Google crawler picks up the links and your site goes up in ranking.

The articles you write and submit should be relevant to your business. They should pertain to what you are doing and whatever business you are in. It doesn't matter what business you are in, article marketing will drive business to your site.

When you are writing articles, they should not only be relevant to your business but should be around 300-500 words long. You want to be picked up as providing good content about your industry or business. You should have a bio attached to the article. This is where the link to your website or splash page will be located. The bio should be about you as the author. The links should only be in your bio, not in the body of the article. This is different than a press release, where the links can be in the body. These links should come back to your website.

Submit at least two articles per week; set aside a specific time or day to make it happen. You have lots of information you can write about in whatever industry you are in. To submit the articles, you can do it manually, or you can purchase submission services through Article Submitter Pro (articlesubmitterpro.com) or Jet Submitter (http://jetsubmitter.com/Article Submitter Pro). They have over 1300 places to submit your articles. It saves you the time from manually submitting articles because it submits the articles for you at a much more rapid pace.

The DNA of Internet Marketing

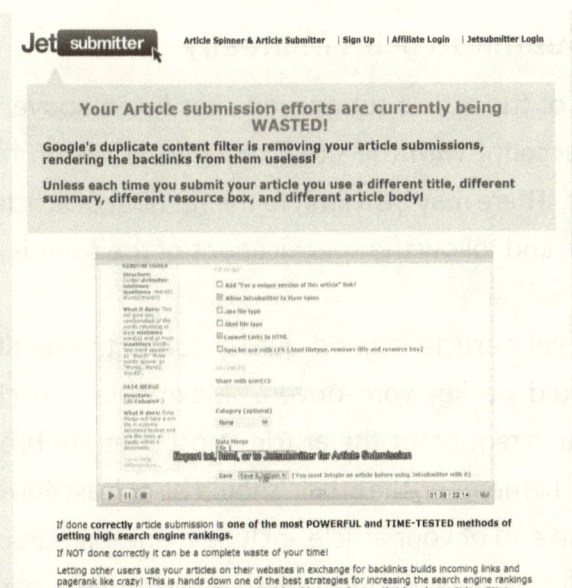

Top Article Locations

www.impactartcles.com

www.isnare.com

www.ezinearticles.com
www.ideamarketers.com
www.articlecity.com
www.workathomearticles.net
www.articlesfactory.com
www.marketing-seek.com
www.goarticles.com
www.article-emporium.com
www.article-directory.net
www.published.com
www.articleworld.com
www.businessknowhow.com
www.searchwarp.com

How to Submit Articles Manually

Go to one of the article submission sites listed above. Log in or create an account with the site if required. Click on the "submit article" link. There may be a limit to the number of articles that you can submit, and follow the specifications of the submission site.

Make sure your article is good quality content. The title of your article should be keyword-driven. Make sure you choose the appropriate category for the article (most sites are broken down by articles). Remember, the article should be at least 400-600 words long. At the end of your article, include a one-paragraph bio that includes a link to your website/splash page/squeeze page.

The DNA of Internet Marketing

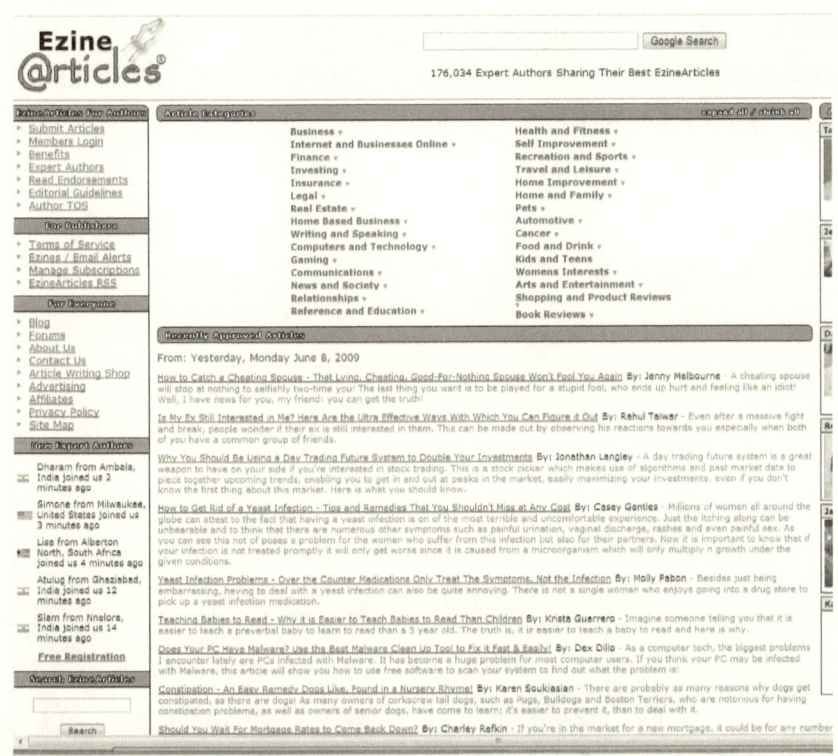

Although all article submission sites vary, they will all be similar. Above is an image of ezine's article submission site. The sites will prompt you for a category, a headline, and allow you to list keywords. Make sure you choose keywords that target your target market. The submission site will also require a summary or abstract...this is where you spend two to three sentences talking about what the article is going to cover. Again, use keywords that attract your target market. In a separate field, the article submission site will allow you to enter your bio, which is where you add a direct link back to your website. Make sure you submit your article to each of the article submission sites listed above.

When Google crawls the sites that pick up your articles, if you are submitting two articles every week and they get picked up by various content sites, your rankings will climb. To be successful, you need to be consistent. Submit two 400- 600-word articles each week. The article will do you no good if there is not an attached bio with a link. If you don't want to submit articles manually, think about getting Article Submitter Pro.

Chapter Five

Video Marketing and Podcasting

Video marketing is the fastest growing and most powerful tool that you have available in your online marketing arsenal. It has proven to be one of the best ways to reach the first page on places like Google, Yahoo, and MSN search engines. Your ultimate goal in marketing is to have your ads not only seen by as many potential customers as possible, but to be in front of as many of your targeted customers as possible. Video marketing is the fastest *free* way to get those ads out there. If you are not using video in your marketing, you will be left behind!

What you are doing with your video marketing is no different than with other forms of internet marketing: your focus should be on specific, target-market driven keywords. We've talked about establishing a target market and a core group of keywords. These same keywords will be plugged into the videos when you submit them. As you can see, everything plays off of your initial development of your target market and core keywords.

You can see what I mean by going to the internet and running a search. Run a search on something like red bicycles. Most likely, in addition to articles and websites, there will be several videos that pop up in the search results. Just think of how powerful a selling tool your video marketing can be if someone types in a search term related to your industry and doesn't just get sent to a splash page but to a dynamic and powerful video that introduces your product, service, and company. Google loves videos and will index them very quickly.

Videos can be done several different ways. Types of video marketing include:

- Actual video of you in front of the camera talking about your product or service
- Power point presentation turned into a video and submitted online
- Even pictures can be transformed into a video that can be submitted online

When submitting videos, as with all other marketing efforts, you are still focused on your target market. How you do that with videos is pretty simple. You do it just like all the other forms of marketing that we have discussed. You will use the same set of keywords that you created while establishing your target market.

These keywords will be submitted at each place that you submit your video. So now, when people do a search on the internet using your keyword, your ad will appear as related to what that end user is looking for. There are a few ways that you can submit your videos on the internet as well as several places you can submit them.

Ways to Submit Video Marketing on the Internet

Manual Submission. You go to each of the places that take video submissions and manually submit you videos. (This is free but takes a long time). Here is a list of places you can submit your videos:

- Google Video
- BrightCove
- PhotoBucket
- Viddler
- YouTube
- DailyMotion
- iFilm
- Myspace
- Vimeo
- BuzzNet
- Flixya
- GoFish
- Kwego
- Lulu
- MyHeavy
- PutFile
- StupidVideos
- Vmix
- ZippyVideos
- CastPost
- Dotv
- Famster

- MeraVideo
- PorkoIt
- VideoWebTown
- Vidmax

Video Submission Programs – There are several programs that will submit your videos for you. These programs will submit your videos to several places on the internet at the same time saving you considerable time and energy. There are two programs I think are the best to use to submit multiple videos at one time.

TubeMogul.com – Free submissions

TrafficGeyser.com – Paid program but is by far the best on the market.

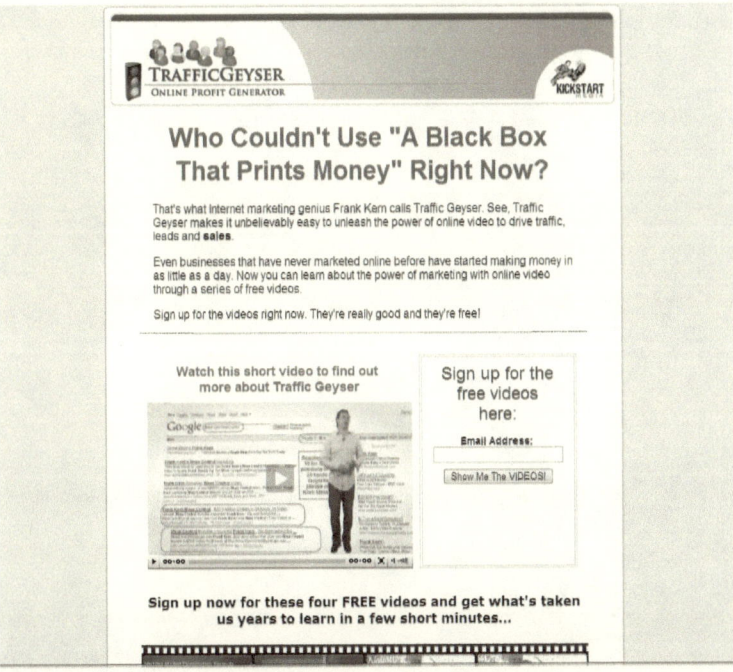

Another way to recycle that same information is to develop podcasts. Take the audio from your video and separate it. Submit the audio to iTunes as a podcast. You'll be marketing to your same core target market. If you have difficulty loading podcasts, see my chapter on outsourcing, because it is something you can hire out very cheaply. All you need to do is sign up for an iTunes account.

Ultimately, what you are trying to do is make sure that anyone who is searching for information in your industry or niche is driven to you. Not only does this establish you as a reliable expert in your industry but it provides you with enormous numbers of leads to whom you can market your products – leads who already have a genuine interest in what you are offering.

Chapter Six

Press Releases

Press Releases are a very important part of your internet marketing campaign. You should be a monthly activity; you should be doing press releases at least once a month. The information in your press release needs to be viable, newsworthy information. Inside your press release, you should have one-way links that bring readers back to your site – your branding site or your squeeze page.

By including the links back to your branding site or squeeze page, it will improve your ranking. Press releases are a great SEO tool that can quickly improve your ranking. There are a lot of sites looking to gather information to build the content on their websites, so if they pick up your press release, and inside your press release you have one-way links back to your site, the search engines pick that up.

This is not an overnight sensation but builds traffic to your site over time. As long as you do this on a consistent basis, sending out one to five press releases per month with relevant, newsworthy information, you'll start seeing increased traffic to your site. Your page rank will start building and you will start getting a lot of free traffic to your site and free leads, which will cut down the cost of pay per click and article submission.

Just like article marketing, your goal with press releases is to get your information out on the web so you can have those one-way links coming from the Press Release back to your website.

Here is a list of other Press Release locations you can submit to free:

- www.free-press-release.com
- www.prleap.com
- www.clickpress.com
- www.express-press-release.com
- www.prlog.org
- www.afly.com
- www.malebits.com
- www.pressreleasespider.com
- www.pressexposure.com
- www.sanepr.com
- www.prurgent.com
- www.prfree.com
- www.freepressindex.com
- www.transworldnews.com
- www.prbuzz.com
- www.i-newswire.com

While there are many places where you can submit your press releases that are free, I suggest the following paid press release

The DNA of Internet Marketing

services, as they will provide you the most exposure and best ranking very quickly with Google:

1. PR Web – Largest Exposure
2. FastPitch – Highly Targeted Business Professionals (this is a membership site)

I like using PR Web and FastPitch on the paid side of Press Releases as they get you the fastest exposure in the search engines. PR Web and FastPitch are the best paid press release submission sites, reaching as many as **50,000** members. When you use PR Web, select the SEO Visibility Package – $200 package for best exposure; when you use FastPitch, their $195 package is the best choice.

PR Web

FastPitch

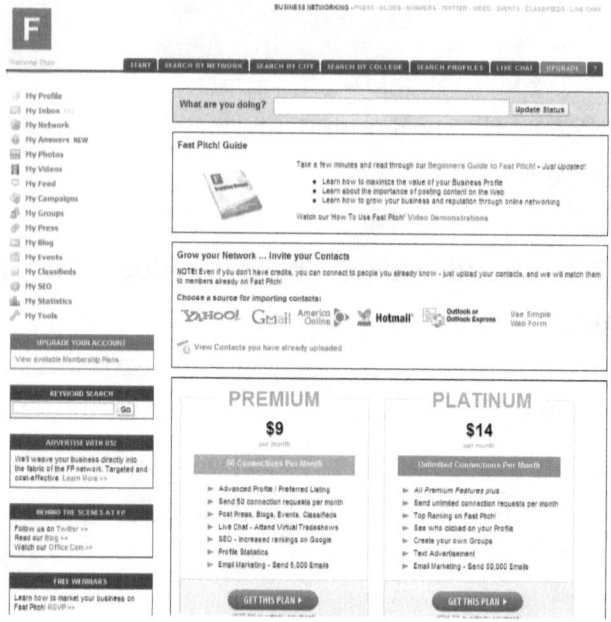

These packages allow you to use the SEO techniques we recommend, like including the one-way link to your site. When other sites pick up the press release from PR Web and FastPitch, they put a one-way link on their website to your website. When the search engines crawl, they pick up your links and ramp up your rankings.

PR Web is the largest press release submission site and will probably get you the best results, so start with them. You need to provide good content if you want it to get picked up so that you can build your page rank value and free traffic to your site.

How to Write a Press Release

When you are entering your Press Release, it is a little different when it comes to adding the links in your Press Release. In the articles, we put the links in the Bio, but in the Press Release, we will put the links in the body of the Press Release. When submitting your press releases, you will also be entering in some keywords for the search engines. Just like I discussed when establishing your target market, you need to use those keywords when submitting your Press Release as well. There will be a box to add keywords to during the process of your press release submission.

Every press release has a headline that targets your market. The summary is a quick-hit description of the information contained in the press release and should draw interest. The body of the press release will have links back to your site. A rule of thumb is that for each 100 words in your press release you can have a link back to your site.

Whatever words you want to be a hyperlink going back to your site need to be inside brackets. The destination URL, including the http://, should appear before the bracketed information. The instructions for including the hyperlink are easily accessed at PR Web's website. When you build the hyperlink, your actual website will not show up, but the words you want to appear (the ones inside the brackets) will.

For example, inside your press release, you will write:

XYZ Company's http://www.lehmanhaily.com [Trade Secret DVD] is now available to the general public.

The way this will appear in the press release when it is published is:

XYZ Company's Trade Secret DVD is now available to the general public.

The instructions on the site are clear and easy to follow, so you should have no trouble building your press release. There is even a spell check tool. Under the press release, you will have the opportunity to choose keywords you want to tie to your press release. You can select all the keywords that you want to drive traffic to your press release. Finally, you will choose the categories that fit your industry and the press release. You can add as many categories as fit to your business.

You can also target the location to which you want your press release to be targeted. You can choose specific locations or broadcast your press release worldwide. You will then be prompted to add your website, location, contact information, and then click "submit."

Once you have live press releases on PR Web, you can use the tools they have available on their site to see how much traffic you are generating. You can see how many people have clicked on your press release, how many have downloaded it, and other helpful tools that help you measure the effectiveness of your press release. To see these stats, click on release visibility and then click on summary. It breaks down how many times the press release was downloaded and in what format, how many search engine hits it had (even broken down by search engine), and which countries and locations.

Press releases are a very effective way to increase your page ranking and well worth the $400 marketing budget. It is a very valuable tool for getting your website out there to generate quality traffic to your website and improve your ranking.

Chapter Seven

Web 2.0 and Social Marking Sites

Web 2.0 is a big craze and gives you another way to drive traffic to your site. Social networking sites like Facebook, Twitter, MySpace, and others are taking the internet by storm. Other Web 2.0 sites that are worth exploring are YouTube, Squidoo, Gizmoz, and Social Bookmarking. Millions of people everyday are viewing, updating, or connecting with others all over the world. These sites are very easy to get set up on, as all you have to do is sign up with your information and you are ready.

Some of these places have built in blogs, forums, groups, places to put banners and more. As of today the big three that I use consistently for internet marketing are Facebook, Twitter, and MySpace. There are hundreds more out there and this is a great way to let people know about who you are, what you do, as well as what your product or service is all about.

Here are some examples of social networking sites:

Lehman Hailey

FaceBook

Twitter

MySpace

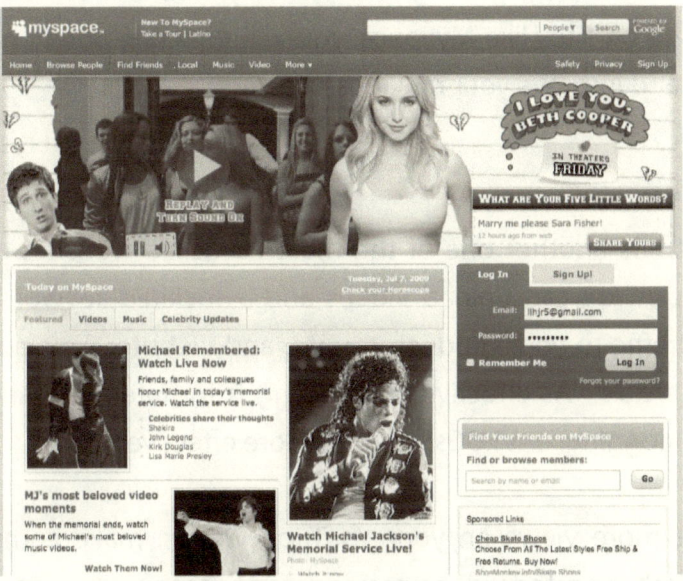

MySpace is one of the most trafficked website, period. I have heard that if you took the people on MySpace and put them in a country, it would be the 12th largest country in the world. It's simple to join; you just need an email address. Once you build a profile, you can begin joining groups, posting on friends' profiles, and posting bulletins every week. MySpace has forums; the average age of Myspace users is 36-45. It's a great place to connect with your target market.

MySpace is not just for kids or teenagers. It's a great place for marketing your business. You should create a profile for your business. Regardless of what industry you are in, you can use MySpace to market. The most important tool on MySpace is the blog. I use my MySpace blog on a regular basis. Within your blog, you can embed one-way links back to your branding site or squeeze page. MySpace is a huge website with top ranking on all of the search engines. By putting your one-way links that come back to your site on sites like MySpace, you will generate additional free traffic and improve your rankings.

YouTube

YouTube is another one of the most trafficked websites on the internet. You can upload videos and associated keywords that drive traffic to your product, service, and website. You can host commercials. As effective as blogging is for internet marketing, video blogging, or VLOGs are even more effective.

To get more views on your YouTube videos, make comments about other posted videos, provide video response to videos, and bookmark your videos using social bookmarking. This is a great way to drive traffic back to your site.

Squidoo

Google loves this site. It's a great place to get more video up. It's easy to set up a site; it's free to build a profile. This has become one of the places to go when wanting to get free content out on the web about you, your product, or service.

Social Bookmarking

This is a great way to get more traffic and backlinks to your site. If you are on a limited budget, social bookmarking is something you should be doing every week. Social bookmarking sites include:

- Del.icio.us
- Reddit.com
- StumbleUpon.com

Use these social bookmarking sites to bookmark your favorite sites. Obviously, your branding site and squeeze page should be your favorite sites. They will grow in popularity the more you have people coming to your sites. It's a great way to generate free traffic. Many of these social bookmarking sites will allow you to post videos and put more content about yourself, your videos, your squeeze pages, and your branding sites. If you don't have a very high marketing budget, you should be starting with these free accounts.

Gizmoz

This is a great website for gadgets for your website and the fastest way to get your personalized video on your website. Gizmoz has powerful utilities and another way to get traffic to your site. There are millions of people using these sites and by being involved in them, you can attract more traffic back to your site for no additional cost.

Gizmoz is my least favorite of the Web 2.0 sites, because it deals in animation, but for many people it is the right choice, and it does work. You can explore the site and see if the tools will work for you. You can put content on the site as well as one-way links back to your site.

Blogging

A lot of people overlook blogging, think it's just a journal. It is an online journal on your website. But it is important to internet marketing. Blogging does help build your page ranking for your website.

You need to be blogging at least three times a week. You can blog about anything, but make sure it's sprinkled with keywords that are relevant to your business. You should have new things to talk about every day. Write a paragraph about your industry and sprinkle it with keywords.

Let's say you are in sports equipment sales. You can blog about sporting news; watch ESPN and report on the action. Tie it back to the services and products you provide.

Where to Get a Blogging Account

www.blogger.com
www.wordpress.com
www.blogspot.com

I recommend, however, that you build a website with either Wordpress or Droople where your blog can be attached to your website. Blogs that are attached to your website, when Google's spiders come and crawl through your site, the activity from your blog will provide additional content that allows your website's rank to increase. Google and the other search engines are trying to provide the most relevant content to their customers who are making the searches. By having your blog connected to your website, it will improve your ranking more quickly.

What you need to do is make sure you are blogging at least three times a week, talking about topics relevant to your product or industry. If you have a squeeze page or branding site, you can embed a one-way link back to that page from your blog. Not only will you generate additional leads but you will also increase your site's ranking through blogging.

Blogging is a free tool for internet marketers that has huge potential for driving additional traffic to your site when done correctly. It's a great way to build your search engine optimization because you are building content on your site. When you think you don't have anything to write about, study your industry. The blog entries do not have to be long; but make sure the information you are writing is meaningful content.

The great thing about blogs is that your readers can subscribe to them. When they subscribe, they'll be notified when you add a new entry. The more times the subscribers come back to your blog, the more opportunity you have to get their information and build your leads. If you don't like writing, you can outsource this job quickly and easily, so don't let that stop you from building a blog.

***

You should be dedicating a couple of hours a week to building your profiles on these Web 2.0 sites. These are great tools for internet marketing that do not cost you anything but can build a great deal of traffic back to your site, build credibility, as well as improve your search engine ranking.

When posting to these social networking sites, you should always have a link back to your web page. You always want to have the opportunity to capture their information (Name and Email) so that you have them in your database for future marketing.

Chapter Eight

Outsourcing

Everything that you have learned in this book, every tool that you use can be outsourced. You simply have to determine how much your time is worth. If you are someone who doesn't like to write articles, press releases, or blogs, you can outsource it. If you don't like doing web design or building squeeze pages, outsource it.

Look, you've probably come to the point where you are working on the internet because you've made a choice to have more free time, to have time to spend with your family. You may have even purposely walked away from the corporate world. So why would you waste that time doing some of the menial tasks associated with internet marketing if you can have someone else do them for you? There are places you can go to get just about anything done for you at a very good price that keep you from being chained to your computer doing all of the work yourself. Find out what you are good at doing, and do it. Outsource the rest.

Let me give you an example of how this works. You have a job to be done, for example, a website that you want to have designed. You can go to several places and post a job that need to be done. You will give your job a title as well as exactly what you are wanting, and people from around the world will bid on your job. It is much like E-bay but opposite.

People on E-Bay bid on products and the price of the product go up until the highest bidder takes the prize. When you place jobs on outsourcing sites, professionals bid the job down. It is up to you to select the person that you want to work with.

Places To Post You Jobs (Work You Need Done):

- Scriptlance.com
- Guru.com
- Elance.com
- Rentacoder.com
- Agentsofvalue.com (this is a company where you can hire people from overseas full or part time to work for you)

Explore these websites. I recommend scriptlance first, then guru. I seem to have the most success with the professionals associated with those sites.

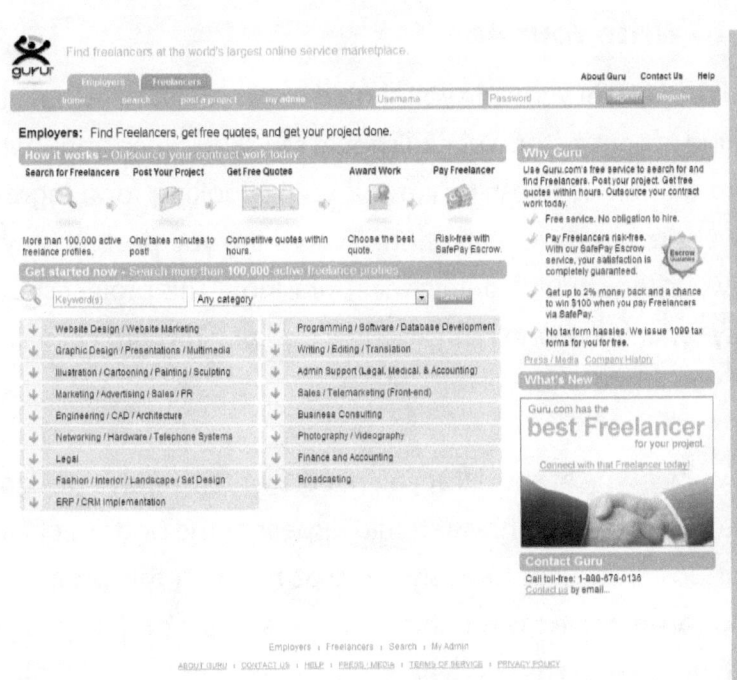

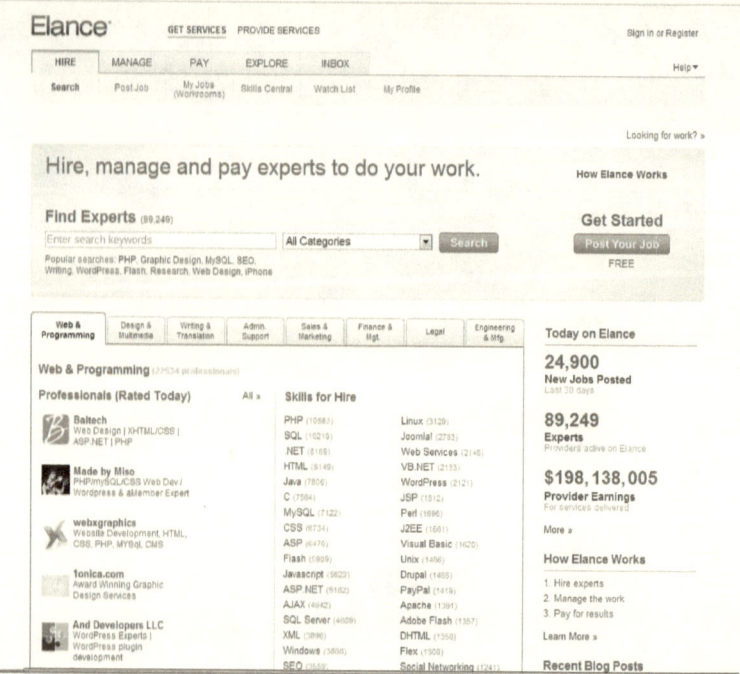

How to Write Your Ad

There is important verbiage you should use in your ad to attract the right kind of contractor. Your ad should say, "Easy if you know what you are doing." It doesn't matter if you're looking for a logo for your website or article marketing. Everything you post, on any of these websites, should contain that phrasing. "This project should be easy for anyone who has experience…" or, "This project will be easy if you know what you are doing."

Specify what type of specialist you need…writer, graphic designer, website builder. This phrase should appear at the bottom of each of your posts. Studies have shown that by using this phrase not only do you increase the number of bidders on the project, but you tend to get a better deal.

Another phrase that is important is to mention that the project is to "clone" something that has already been done. For example, if you want a website designed and there is a website out there that you want to emulate, you can advertise on your outsourcing ad that you are looking to "clone a website."

What Can You Outsource?

Anything that has to do with internet marketing can be outsourced, from building your pages to writing and submitting articles and press releases. Customer support and accounting functions can be outsourced. Web design and graphics arts...basically everything you need for your business can be outsourced.

How Do You Post a Project?

The first thing you will need to do is create an account with whichever site you choose. You'll be assigned a username and password, which you can use to log in to the site. When you need to hire someone, you simply post a project. You can choose how long the project is posted, what categories the job posts to, and the budget range of the project. I never post a budget range, however; I wait and let the professionals tell me how much they'll charge.

Type in the description of your job, including the recommended phrase. You can attach information to the job posting, but I don't recommend it. I only send that information to the person to whom I've awarded the project. You can pay extra to feature the job or make it private, but I don't do either. Once you've completed creating the project, just click "submit project."

Outsourcing Tips

Most of the sites, like guru and scriptlance, have specific rules about how you contact professionals. Make sure you read through the rules and regulations for the outsourcing sites you.

As well, you should never choose the lowest bidder just because it's a low bid. Make sure the person you choose is actually capable of providing the services you are requesting. Ask to see samples or review their profile. Most sites have some kind of ranking system that is visible to you. Make sure the person you are hiring does not have a bunch of negative feedback from previous employers.

What's Your Job?

You should spend time obtaining specialized knowledge in your field or industry. Build yourself into a credible expert. Create a system, become a contractor. Delegate.

If you find someone who does good work for you, keep them. Pay them well. Treat them right. You'll get better work from them.

When to Hire

I'll probably never hire anyone in house. For me, outsourcing is too convenient and gives me access to the best talent around the world and not just what's in my own community. It also keeps me from having added overhead, because I never have to deal with benefits like health insurance and retirement accounts.

Chapter Nine

Marketing Resources

I hope you are enjoying the book so far and some of these tools and techniques you can use to really get your business out there in front of your target market. *The DNA of Internet Marketing* really hinges on your target market – knowing who your target market really is. There are a lot of tools out there that will shorten your learning curve and assist you in some of the jobs in marketing.

In this chapter, I'm going to share with you a lot of the tools I've used over the past five years in my marketing campaigns in several different businesses. These are tools that I've picked up from different people, tools I've discovered on the internet, in seminars, and workshops…but all of these tools can help you achieve success, save time, and build wealth.

Article Submission Programs

Article Submitter Pro
Jetsubmitter.com

Free Manual Submission Sites for Article Marketing

http://www.impactarticles.com
http://www.isnare.com
http://www.ezinearticles.com
http://www.ideamarketers.com
http://www.articlecity.com
http://www.articlehub.com
http://www.workathomearticles.net
http://www.articlesfactory.com
http://www.goarticles.com
http://www.articlemarketer.com
http://www.published.com
http://www.articleworld.com
http://www.businessknowhow.com
http://searchwarp.com

PRESS Release Submission Sites - Paid

PRWeb
PRWeb is the best place for submitting Press Releases

Fast Pitch
Fast Pitch is another great place for submitting Press Releases

Press Release Program

pressequalizer.com

More Press Release Sites (Some Are FREE)

www.prleap.com
www.express-press-release.com

www.prnuke.com
www.pressreleasespider.com
www.pressmethod.com
www.pr9.net
www.pressexposure.com
www.sanepr.com
www.prurgent.com
www.prfree.com
www.freepressindex.com
www.transworldnews.com
www.prbuzz.com
www.i-newswire.com
www.press-base.com
www.1888pressrelease.com
www.clickpress.com
www.free-press-release.com

Below is a list of places on the internet where you can market your business product or service. These places allow various types of advertising. When you visit the site for the first time, you will need to be looking for the small link that says "Advertise" or "Advertise Here." Click on that link for the advertising details that are associated with that particular site. These sites allow various types of advertising so you will need to look into each site for the details on what type of advertising they accept (Pay Per Click, Banner Placement, Article Submission, Classified Ads, E-Mail Marketing, Ezine Ads, and much more).

Advertising List

1. http://www.DotComMOmmies.com
   Media Types: article, advertical, text ad, link, newsletter, solo email, button, banner, directory

2. http://www.yahoo.com
   Media Types: banner, pop ups, online classified, job listing

3. http://www.imagevenue.com
   Media Types: banner

4. http://www.veoh.com
   Media Types: banner

5. http://www.ezboard.com
   Media Types: banner, print classified, online classified, ffa

6. http://www.zango.com
   Media Types: banner, button, text ad, popup, popover

7. http://www.yellowpages.com
   Media Types: listing, text ad, banner

8. http://www.tucows.com
   Media Types: banners

9. http://www.johnchow.com
   Media Types: sponsored review, business review, article, advertical, text link, business post, blog, solo email, banner

10. http://www.problogger.net
    Media Types: text links, banner ads, newsletter placements and RSS feed ads

11. http://www.handango.com
    Media Types: banner

12. http://www.yachtworld.com
    Media Types: banner

13. http://www.ryze.com
    Media Types: networking, article, advertical, text ad, text link, banner, button, ezine, newsletter, directory

14. http://www.infoworld.com
    Media Types: banner, text link, email newsletter, podcast

15. http://www.bizbuysell.com
    Media Types: banner, text ad, display ad, classified, business listing

16. http://www.kompass.com
    Media Types: banner, text ad, text link, logo, directory

17. http://www.emarketer.com
    Media Types: banner, text ad

18. http://www.bizland.com
    Media Types: banner, newsletter

19. http://www.bizshots.com
    Media Types: text ad, text link, banner

20. http://www.inetgiant.com
    Media Types: banner, free classifieds, solo email, targeted traffic, guaranteed leads guaranteed signups, search engine optimization

21. http://www.activerain.com
    Media Types: message board, forum

22. http://www.careerbuilder.com
    Media Types: advertical, job posting, newsletter

23. http://www.ryze.com
    Media Types: networking, article, advertical, text ad, text link, banner, button, ezine, newsletter, directory

24. http://www.plugim.com
    Media Types: plug, text ad, advertical

25. http://www.entrepreneurs-journey.com
    Media Types: banner, sponsored review, text link, advertical

26. http://www.ultra-blogs.com
    Media Types: banner, sponsored review, text link, advertical

27. http://www.bizwits.com
    Media Types: banner, text ad, advertical

28. http://www.businesstycoons.org
    Media Types: banner, online classified

29. http://www.sterlingwebtraffic.com
    Media Types: banner, text, paid to click

30. http://www.business-opportunities.biz
    Media Types: banner, adverticle, newsletter

Useful Links

Adbrite
AdBrite, "The Internet's Ad Marketplace," is an e-commerce site. They sell ad space on thousands of websites. It's a great place for banners and other advertising.

Perfect Traffic
Perfect Traffic has packages from $38 and up, with banner placement, slide in banners, pop-ups, guaranteed traffic, text links, and more!

Googspy.com
This site can give you information about your competition and what keywords they are bidding on.

Free Places to Submit Ads

Goezines.com
ezinepublishing.com
ezinesauctions.com
bestezines.com

Auto Responders That You Can Use

aweber.com
constantcontact.com
autoresponceplus.com
icontact.com

Outsourcing

RentaCoder.com
Guru.com

Scriptlance.com
needanarticle.com
Elance.com
Bestjobs.ph (looking for full time outsourcing)

Tracking and Testing

Google Analytics
Hyper Tracker

Video

<u>For PCs</u> (Screen Recording Programs)
Camtasia

<u>For Macs</u> (Screen Recording Programs)
iShowU
Screen Mimic
Screen Flow

Programs for Submitting and Working with Videos

Traffic Geyser – Traffic Geyser is a paid service that submits to a ton of video locations; it's not cheap but well worth it.

Tube Mogul - Free video submission service that will submit you videos to several sharing sites.

animoto.com - another great place to create videos

avs4you.com - Free Video Converter

Places to get a Domain and Hosting

NameCheap.com

Lizardhosting.com (Hosting)

RhinoDaddy.com (They host sites as well)

HostGator.com (They host sites as well)

Bonus Chapter

Russell Brunson: Fire First, Aim Later

My name is Russell Brunson. I started my business about seven years ago while I was wrestling at Boise State University. I had just gotten married to my beautiful wife, and because I was wrestling and going to school and we had just gotten married, we didn't have a lot of money. My wife made about $10 an hour, and since I went to school during the day and wrestled at night, I didn't have a job.

I always felt kind of guilty as the husband; I was supposed to be the provider for our family, so I went to the internet to see if I could find a way to make some money, and that's where I got started. I spent about a year and a half to two years trying to figure out how to make money online. I tried everything; I fell for almost every scam out there and lost a lot of money that we didn't have to lose, and finally I stumbled upon a very simple model to make money on the internet, which is basically to create an information product, a simple website, and then drive traffic to the site to sell that product.

I started doing that. I made one product and made a bunch of sales, then created a second and third product and kept growing and growing. By my senior year in college, I'd made about $250,000 that year; within a year of graduating from college I'd made my millionth dollar and this year – my company has been in business for over three years – my company will do well over ten million dollars.

We just took that same simple system and process and kept growing and building it over and over again. Internet business and the whole concept is something I've become very passionate about. I study and I learn and I teach and I do; it's very fun.

Lehman asked me what I would do if I had to start over again with no money, knowing what I know now, to get back on top of the industry. That's kind of a fun question for me right now because I'm actually actively in the process with a new company I've just launched in a different industry, and I actually sat down before I launched this new company and said the same thing. What do I need to do to get to the point where I'm making ten million dollars a year with this company? What are the steps I need to have in place?

My main company is called dotcomsecrets.com; if you want to see what we've done there, you can go visit the site to see our internet business. The new company we've launched is called bodyevolution.com, and I'm going to share with you here some of the different things we put in place and why we did it to build the business.

When we created dotcomsecrets, I created myself as the attractive character of the site – the personality that people would communicate through – which was which was good for a lot of reasons, but it was also bad for a lot of reasons. It makes it difficult for you to step out of the business; it makes it difficult to sell the business. When we built bodyevolution.com, I didn't want to be the figure person for that company, so we recruited and found people who would be good public faces for the company. We were very lucky, actually, to stumble upon Matt and Suzy Hoover, who were the winners of The Biggest Loser Season 2.

We signed them on to become the attractive characters of our site. What was nice was that we found a man and a woman, both of whom had gone through an amazing body evolutions on the show The Biggest Loser, and we wanted them to be the figure faces of the web site. The nice thing about them as well is that they were already getting a lot of PR and a lot of traffic, which is obviously very strategic for us in picking them to be the face of our website. They already have a name out there so we can build off their existing credibility.

The next step was that we needed some kind of product. Part of the reason I struggled the first 18 months I tried to be in business was because I didn't have a product. Now, through the years I've been doing this, the one thing I've found is that it's always easier to make money without having to sell a product; selling a product can be difficult. What we did for bodyevolutions.com was to create a "free plus shipping" offer – it's an offer that's completely free, you just have to cover shipping and handling. If the customer did that, they were placed in a continuity program, which is like a membership program, where they pay $30, $40, or $50 a month and they pay continuously until they cancel.

The nice thing about free plus shipping offers is it gives you something cool to advertise, something cool to talk about. For example, Matt and Suzy were on the show the 700 Club, and during the show, they were able to say, "If you ever want a free DVD where you can learn the stuff we're talking about, just go to bodyevolution.com and you can get your free DVD." It's very easy for them to pitch and to promote; there were a lot of people watching that TV show that came to our site to get a free DVD.

Matt and Suzy can do the same thing when they are posting in forums or through pay per click and all the other forms of advertising we choose to do. It's a lot easier to advertise a free DVD or a free CD than it is to convince someone to buy your product.

I also wanted to make sure we had a cash flow from day one from that company. One of the biggest mistakes I made when I first got started on the Internet was that I didn't focus on cash flow. I focused on products – I would create a product, launch it, make some money; create another product launch it, make some money – but there was no consistent cash flow coming from them. So this time around, launching this new company, I wanted to have cash flow from day one. I needed to have enough money to pay Matt and Suzy, to pay the other people working on it, so I needed cash flow as quick as possible. That's why, from day one, we built in the continuity program into our free plus shipping offer.

The next thing, and this is one of the biggest keys I hope I can give you, what I hope you will take away from this, is that starting even before we launched the company, we started building relationships with experts in the industry. The key is to find people who already have lists, who already have existing customers, customers we are trying to get. We wanted to make sure that we had built relationships with those kinds of people, the experts in the industry, so that when we were ready, they could help us launch our product.

One of the biggest mistakes that most people make when they get into any kind of industry is they create their product and create their business and then go and try to find partners to help promote it. The problem with that is that people like to promote people that they know, they like, and they trust. If your first conversation with these people is "Hey I've got a new product I'd like you to promote," it's very difficult to get that person to actually go and promote it.

That's why we spend a lot of time building relationships, getting to know people, finding out how we can work with them, because if we can get one or two good relationships – one or two good people with whom we can build that relationship ahead of time – then when our product is ready, it's much easier to come back and have them promote it.

So for the last five or six months before we even launched the new company, we've spent a lot of time getting to know people, developing relationships with experts in the industry, and helping them out, so that when we were ready to launch, we had these people on board and we already had a relationship. That's really one of the keys to getting to the top of the industry fast is the relationships you build – networking, going to events, getting to know the players in the field – those are ways to help you propel and launch your product and business very, very quickly. That was how we were able to take a company like bodyevolution.com off the ground, where no one knew who we were, and within a few weeks to a month, we have a thriving business that's bringing in thousands and thousands of dollars a day, giving us something we can build off of and grow a big business.

Hopefully, this approach will help you shortcut your route. A lot of you are probably going the slower approach, where you've created a product and now you're trying to drive some pay per click traffic, trying some SEO, and slowly going through the process. If you really want to fast track it and get to the top of the industry quickly, the keys are very simple:

1. Creating a free plus shipping product
2. Having a good continuity program in place
3. Building solid, strong relationships with people who already have existing businesses, who already have the customers that you want, who already have a herd of people that you would like access to. Build those relationships and then go and drive traffic through them.

That's really how the process works. Those are really the steps that I would focus on, and then long term from there is to realize that you really shouldn't focus on just a product. A lot of people focus on a product; they fall in love with it. Most of our products are free plus shipping type offers. The reason for this type of offer is because I can develop them very quickly; I can think of a unique angle for each of these products; I can promote the product and sell it and get a lot of traffic and a lot of sells very quickly.

If you focus too much on one product and invest all your time in making that one product successful, you may end up not being successful, because you're focused too much on that one thing. What we do is develop a free plus shipping offer tied to a continuity program, and then we'll develop a second free plus shipping offer that has a different angle or different twist and we'll hook it to the same continuity program. Then we'll create yet a third offer for the same continuity program.

For example, for bodyevolution.com, our first free plus shipping offer was about Matt and Suzy. We actually took a video camera, went to their house, and showed people how they live their life now that they're off the show. That was our free DVD. A lot of people were interested. Our next DVD will probably be something about Matt and Suzy talking about how they work out with their kids, or how they eat the right way, or how they get themselves psychologically in the state of mind where they can lose weight. It can be any different angle, just a lot of little front end offers to hook them into the same continuity program, giving new offers and products that people can go and promote to their lists.

So that's the way that I'd get back on top as quick as possible without having to spend a lot of time or energy or money developing a huge business, just developing the simple easy parts and then building off of there.

My final advice to anybody who is out there trying to build a business, one of my favorite quotes – in fact I have a big sign with it above my desk – says "Ready, Fire, Aim." The biggest problem people have when they're trying to get started and trying to build a business and get high in their industry is that they are focusing so much on aiming and getting things perfect that they never fire. They keep aiming, and aiming, and aiming, but they never fire.

So I say shift your focus around, get ready, go and fire and try something and fail and fail fast and fail over and over and over again and get the failures out of the way as quick as possible because they're going to come – you're going to make mistakes, you're going to have problems. But if you keep sitting there aiming and trying to perfect something, you're never going to be successful with it, so go out there ready, fire, aim…take that approach; do not be afraid of failure, realize you're going to fail, tell people you're planning on failing, just don't worry about that piece of it.

Just worry about getting it out there and if it works, improve upon it and perfect it but don't focus on that part of it until it's out there and it's working and you've got something to show. That's really the key is moving fast on these things. Joe Vitale told me one time, he said, "Money follows speed." And it's very true…the faster you can get out with things the more money will be attracted to them.

I hope my advice helps you to build your business very quickly and helps you get to the top of your industry as quickly as possible.

Bonus Chapter – How To Get $50,000/Mo In Online Advertising For Free...

By Mike Dillard

Mike Dillard has built the most popular websites and written the best selling courses in the home business industry. Over 100,000 web pages and videos have been posted about Mike online by other people, which is a remarkable testament to his success.

Mike is a close friend of mine, and I asked him to share with my readers the secrets of his success...Specifically, I asked Mike to share what he would do today, knowing everything he knows now, if he was just starting his first online business.

Hey thanks for asking me Lehman, and what a great question!

So what's the answer? How would I go from $0.00, to making 7-figures again if I had to start over from scratch, without a list or any name recognition?

Simple.

I'd do exactly what I did last time, way back in 2004. Pay attention, because this is an extremely unique approach that you've probably never considered.

The life-blood of any business is new prospects or leads.

You need to be able to produce a minimum of 20-30 new leads every single day if you want to make any kind of money in this industry.

The big guys who are making $50,000 per month or more generally produce 100-300 leads per day.

But producing leads generally costs a lot of money. Thankfully, the solution I'm about to show you solves that problem in a very unique way!

So if were low on cash, the first thing we need to do is acquire some VALUE, in the form of a skill set, because if you don't have any money, and you don't have any knowledge or skills, than you're basically worthless to everyone, including yourself.

We'll do that by mastering some new skills as quickly as possible.

The first thing I would master is "pay-per-click," (PPC), or commonly known as "Google Adwords."

This kind of online advertising is the single most powerful form of marketing ever created by man. Nothing else in the world offers as much flexibility, and pin-point accuracy as PPC.

There are dozens of training courses available online that will teach you how to master PPC. Two of my favorites are Perry Marshall's (www.PerryMarshall.com), and Jim Yaghi's "PPC Domination" (www.MagneticSponsoring.com). Jim is my personal Adwords guru.

It will probably cost you around $200-$500 in courses and 90 days to master PPC.

And when I say "master" PPC, I mean that you're able to produce as many leads as you want using this medium, and that you could write your own book on the subject.

But you're still low on money, so how can leverage your new skill and turn it into leads and cash?

Well in 2004, when I was learning all of these skill sets but not making any money yet, I went to the guys in my upline and offered to run a PPC campaign for them, using their money to fund it.

Using free tools like Google Website Optimizer, you can easily rotate every visitor to a different person's capture page.

So let's say that John, Bill, and Sarah joined the co-op, and each gave me $2,000 per month to put towards the PPC campaign.

I now have $6,000 to fund the campaign.

All of the traffic produced was evenly distributed to the three co-op participants using a simple tool called Google Optimizer.

So if I was able to produce 1,200 leads for the $6,000, each participant would have gotten 400 leads at a cost of $5.00 each.

Everyone wins.

My upline was able to leverage my PPC skills in order to provide them with more leads without spending their time on the campaign. I was able to master my PPC skills without spending my money.

Once I had mastered PPC, I started marketing this "lead co-op" as a turnkey system that was only available to the people who joined my downline.

"If you join my team, you can participate in our lead co-op and I'll do all of your marketing for you."

This was an extremely attractive offer, and people started joining my downline by the dozens.

All of a sudden, we had $10,000… $20,000… $50,000… of other people's money coming into the co-op.

And THIS is how you get rich my friend… Leverage. You get to leverage all of this money, and all of these leads being produced, because all of the co-op participants are in your downline.

Imagine what your business could do if you had people in your downline actively spending $30,000-50,000 per month on advertising that you manage.

That's what I would do all over again if I had to start over today. I would learn PPC; I'd put together a co-op; I'd market that co-op; I'd run the co-op. I would get other people's money involved, and I'd leverage all of that. It would all come into my downline. I hope this is a light-bulb idea for you that helps you start to look at a bigger picture that's always outside the box.

Bonus Chapter

Howie Schwartz

Howie Schwartz is an expert internet marketer who has helped thousands of people make money online. He is considered an affiliate marketing guru, famous for his program Howie's Apprentice, a training program where he takes a small group of students, turns them into internet affiliate marketing wizards, and teaches them how to be successful online.

I asked Howie to share his story with my readers, to share his tips for success. This bonus chapter contains Howie's valuable advice about how to build your online business and be the most successful version of yourself.

Howie's Rules

1. **Take It Seriously.** Whatever your online business endeavor is, take it seriously. Treat it as a business, not a hobby. Have a game plan – know what you need to do, how much you need

to make, and be determined to reinvest as much as possible in the business. Know yourself and your strengths.

2. **It All Starts With One Website.** You have to have a product or service to sell and a website to sell it on. That's where it starts. You can't be out there trying every "get rich quick" online business scheme you see. Pick something that you know about, some niche in which you can become a relevant expert, and stay focused.

3. **Use Clickbank or Paypal.** People are much more willing to do business online than they used to be, but you need to have a way to process credit card payments. Clickbank and Paypal are two of the best options; be sure to set up the accounts in the name of the corporation or business entity you create.

4. **Find a Good Mentor.** There is nothing more important than a good mentor when you are an online business entrepreneur. It's easy to get distracted with the many choices out there, but you should find one reliable and trustworthy mentor to rely on. Mentors are people who can help you be successful. They are people who want you to be successful and inspire you.

5. **Take Prep Time Before You Launch.** To be successful, don't rush the process. It's worth the couple of weeks you might be delayed. Take the time to do it right. Incorporate your business. This will protect you and your personal property from being considered if there is a lawsuit; it makes it easier to sell the business down the road when you need to change what you are doing. Get a tax ID number. Keep your business expenses separate from your personal expenses. Get a credit card in your business name.

6. **Know What You Need to Survive.** You may have the entrepreneurial spirit but have a family who relies on you for support. There is risk involved in starting your own business. Make sure you know how much money you need to pay your bills each month. Include everything, including one-time expenses like your daughter's sweet sixteen birthday party or the college expenses you'll be paying in a couple years. Think about the hidden costs of living – things like health insurance (which can cost $500-1000 per month for a family).

7. **Build a Budget.** Using Excel (my preference) or a software program of your choice, build a budget for your business. Consider all of your costs, from advertising to internet. Don't go out and charge your advertising budget to your credit card if you don't know how you are going to repay it, but figure out how much you can afford to invest. If you do choose to use a credit card so that you can start your business more rapidly, have a payment plan for the card.

8. **Reinvest in Your Business.** It's tempting to spend your first profits on a new widescreen TV or a car, but truly successful people reinvest what they can back into the business. It's not about being flashy or showing off your wealth, it's about building a stronger, more stable business so that the wealth will continue. It's not even really about money – it's about freedom. The freedom to work your own hours and do what you want to do; the freedom to spend time with your family, to travel, to unchain yourself from that corporate desk.

9. **Make To-Do List.** Make lists of the things you need to do. Prioritize and stay organized. Working for yourself takes discipline, and you need to be willing to work. Yes, it gives

you the freedom to take a day off and take your kids to the zoo, but you have to spend time with your business if you want it to succeed.

10. **Read About Other People's Success.** Knowing about other successful entrepreneurs can help keep you motivated, so read and learn about the successful men and women you admire. Don't be afraid to learn from their mistakes and mimic their formulas for success.

11. **Have Plan B.** Don't assume you're going to fail, but plan for your worst-case scenario. Have money in the bank to cover the bills. Have a back-up plan ready in case your product or business idea doesn't launch as successfully as you expect it to. Know what you will do next. Know how much risk you can afford to take.

12. **Build Your Skills.** You may be able to afford to outsource building your website and setting up your internet marketing, but you should have some basic web skills, whether you take a community college class or rely on a book. You should know how to set up email accounts, how to create and maintain a basic webpage, how to use your FTP, how to go in and fix a typo on your website or change the title of your sales page. You don't have to be an expert, but you should have some working knowledge.

13. **Put Money in the Bank.** You should have three to six months savings, although there is nothing wrong with having a year or two of income in the bank. Business cycles fluctuate, the economy can and does occasionally tank, so have enough money in the bank that you can ride out the rough times.

14. **Don't Depend on One Traffic Source.** Diversify your business. Once you are up and running and have a handle on what you are doing, work toward developing multiple income streams. By having multiple products and income types, you can weather difficult times more easily.
15. **Stay Positive.** When you first start working for yourself, many of your friends and family members may give you a hard time or accuse you of just sitting around all day. Knowing there are others going through what you are going through can keep you from giving up. Build friendships and partnerships with other online entrepreneurs. Go to seminars, network with people. Negativity will take away from your ability to be successful, so you have to be able to surround yourself with people who believe in your ability to succeed.

Conclusion

Take Action!

Let's recap what we've covered so far in the book. We start out by establishing our target market – knowing exactly who our customer is, where they live, what they do, how they do things, who they hang out with, where they look on the internet – everything you can know about your target market. The more questions you can come up with about who your target market is will really enhance the quality of the leads you're going to be getting because you're really honing in on the exact person you are marketing to.

We talked about developing a squeeze page and branding site. The Squeeze page is the most effective way of capturing information, but after your squeeze page is up and running, I'd turn to developing your branding site. You will need both.

Once we establish that target market, know exactly who we're marketing to, and have a squeeze page to send them to, we take that set of information, that set of keywords and key phrases and apply it to our marketing methods.

Start off with Google, Yahoo, and MSN Pay Per Click marketing. You're looking for instant gratification – and that's what pay per click is, instant gratification. You put an ad on the internet, a little 3-line classified ad, and within minutes – no more than 15 minutes – you're getting leads coming in and you could be getting traffic to your site. It's instant gratification. You are able to compete with the big corporations. Doing it the right way, you are able to compete with large companies, getting traffic and clients to your sites. You are driving customers to your site the same day, right off the bat fast. Instant gratification marketing. Pay per Click. Google, Yahoo, MSN. You turn it on and it starts working for you. It's the best place to start.

Now, we can't just focus on short-term marketing like PPC. We need to be planning for the long haul so let's talk about how we insure that we are seen by the masses for a long period of time. Earlier in the book, we discussed other types of marketing like Article marketing, video marketing, press releases, and web 2.0 sites. These are great ways to focus on the long term efforts in your marketing plan.

Article marketing is great. You should be sending out at least two articles per week and having links coming back to your sites, your squeeze page, your branding site, your Web 2.0 sites. Article marketing is huge. It's really getting good quality content about your product, business, or service out there and having links coming back to your information, your site. It's about boosting your site's rankings with the search engines. Use article submitter pro and jetsubmitter to save time submitting your articles.

Video marketing is also very powerful. Video marketing is more of what we call attraction marketing. It's getting you the person out there where you are the authority on your product or your service or your business. Within those videos that you submit, they also have links that come back to your site where you capture that person's information, so it's a great method of marketing to do video marketing as well. The software you can use in video marketing, Traffic Geyser and Tube Mogul, gets the videos out there. Both the article submitting software and the video submitting software are great tools for getting your information out there quickly without having to spend a lot of time on manual submissions.

Press releases are another great way to get links coming back to your site. It's all about links coming in, about the popularity of your site. We call them votes. The more votes, or links, coming back to your site, the better your ranking with the search engines will be, which is key. You want your website to show up in the natural listings, the free listings on the left hand side of the search page. That's where you want to be…where you are getting free marketing.

We also talked about Web 2.0, social sites like Facebook and Twitter, which are my two favorites. There are a lot of other ones where you can link them together, but I really love Facebook and Twitter.

Outsourcing. We have talked about a lot in this book so far. Everything that we've covered in this book can all be outsourced. I've done all of this before myself, but my time is better served doing things I'm good and efficient at. Building websites is not one of them. Although I can build a website, the time it takes me to do it, I'm actually losing money. The money I'm losing, the time that I'm spending unwisely, could be better spent, and there are tons of people out there who know how to build websites much more quickly and more efficiently than I do.

Article marketing is also easy to outsource. I don't like writing articles that much, so I tend to outsource my writing to someone more skilled and efficient. Quite often, I make audios or videos and have a writer turn that information into an article or press release. I'll voice over a PowerPoint presentation or do a video, and then outsource articles and press releases to be created from that video that I created. This is a great way to use the same material in multiple formats.

A lot of the set up of the Web 2.0 sites and social bookmarking sites I outsource as well. That's just busy work. It isn't the best use of my time.

Find out what you are good at, find out what's going to really make you money, and then outsource the rest of it. Some people don't have the funds to outsource at the beginning, so you're going to have to take this in a step-by-step format. That's why I laid the book out like this, having you establish your target market, build your squeeze page and branding site, and get some instant gratification using pay per click on Yahoo, Google, and MSN in the very beginning, before getting into article and video marketing and the other marketing methods mentioned. Once you get set up, though, I definitely recommend outsourcing.

We covered a lot of the marketing resources that I've used in the last five years. Make sure you take advantage of that; make sure you use those resources, because those are resources I still use today.

Last but not least, we got some really good bonus information from Russell Brunson, Howie Schwartz, and Mike Dillard, as well as from Matt Bacak who wrote the foreword. Pay attention to these guys as well. All four of these guys are people I've really looked up to since getting into this industry. They're people you should be looking up to as well. They have great information.

We've covered a lot of information in this book, but until you do something with it, it doesn't mean anything. One of my favorite quotes is from Tony Robbins. He says that information alone won't change our lives. What we do with the information is what we really matters.

It's the actions we take that ultimately make a difference in our lives.

Make sure you take action on each one of the steps in this book. I hope you enjoyed the book and that it provides you with the tools and resources you need to meet your goals and give you the freedom and wealth you desire.

Please visit my blog at http://www.lehmanhailey.com and give us some feedback on the book. I am there answering all questions concerning internet marketing and building a successful business online. Feel free to visit my site above anytime to submit your internet marketing questions as we are always here to assist you in building a successful online business.

Get your access now to my FREE 10 Day DNA Marketing Boot Camp Videos

Go to http://www.dnamarketingbootcamp.com

www.ingramcontent.com/pod-product-compliance
Lightning Source LLC
Chambersburg PA
CBHW022025170526
45157CB00003B/1351